To

Vanessa

with love and

happiness

Kim
x

Published in 2013 by Marplesi

Copyright © Kim Macleod 2013

ISBN 978-0-9575566-4-5

Cover designed by Marplesi

A catalogue record for this book is available
from the British Library.

From Heartbreak
To Happiness

by

Kim Macleod

Marplesi Books

Dedication

This book is dedicated to my wonderful family. My loving and supportive husband Sinclair, my beautiful, intelligent, kind and caring daughter Kirsten and in memory of my guiding inspiration – my handsome, funny, kind-hearted and loving son Calum.

Acknowledgements

There are so many people to thank who in their own way made this book possible.

The first is my wonderful editor and friend Christine McPherson who had a vision for me writing a book before I thought I could. It may have taken time to get here but it wouldn't have happened without your guidance and encouragement - thank you.

When we experienced the worst time in our lives we were surrounded by family and friends who went out of their way to offer us emotional support and stay with us at the hospital. They continued to help with practical help, encouragement and a shoulder to cry on. I am forever indebted to my mum Margaret and dad Paul, Lynda, Robert and Jane, Andrew and Karen, David and Carolyn, Alan and Lorna, Ann and Keith, Margaret, Robert and Morven, Iain, Larraine, Isla and Emma, May and Osvaldo, and Steve. You all put your own lives on hold to help and then nurtured us back to life again.

Thank you to the wonderful doctors and nurses at the Royal Hospital for Sick Children in Glasgow and the Organ donation team who cared for Calum and us with such compassion.

To the fabulous teachers at Bishopbriggs Academy especially Gordon Moulsdale, Moira Carberry and David

Hepburn. Your efforts to recognise the loss that we felt and support us in all our fundraising efforts was outstanding. Your continued support for Kirsten is also very much appreciated.

To Calum's fabulous friends (and their parents) especially Garry, Marcus, David, Gavin, Graham, Callum, Kevin, Andrew, Rosie, Minnie and Rachel who kept Calum alive in their hearts and minds, raised our spirits and supported Kirsten too. You are a lovely group of people and I wish you long and happy lives.

Thank you to Calum's favourite band – Baz, Jon and Mince Fratelli. You are totally wonderful human beings who have brought many smiles and a connection that means such a lot.

Thank you also to Gino D'Acampo, Calum's favourite TV chef, who reached out and touched our hearts in our darkest hour.

Meningitis Now (formerly the Meningitis Trust) have given us incredible support. Thank you especially to Kerry Ross, Ann Currie and Jo Stevenson for your practical support and for giving us a route to channel our energy and fundraising efforts in Calum's name. Thank you to Sue Davie for all your hard work and for providing some comments for this book.

To everyone who has helped in our fundraising efforts I thank you. I know that the hill climbs, the bike rides, swims, runs, book sales, sponsored events, fire walks, concerts and all the other events were done with Calum in your heart.

To all of our extended family, friends and neighbours who have spent time sharing their lives with us I thank you. The chats, cups of tea, smiles and friendship offered to us continue to enrich our lives.

I also want to thank Action for Happiness for being a catalyst in helping me to create a route for my passion and for their ongoing support and encouragement.

For the members of the Happiness Club, thank you for sharing your happiness with me.

Thank you to Sinclair, my soul mate, you are a wonderful man and I love you very much. I look forward to sharing many more happy years together. This book would not have been possible if it wasn't for your encouragement and skill in putting it all together to become a real book.

To Kirsten, I love you so very much, which I know will be a bit mushy for a teenager. You gave me a reason to keep going when life was so bleak and give me a reason to smile every day. I am so very proud of you.

My last acknowledgement is for Calum, thank you - you gave me almost 13 years of sheer love and joy. I wouldn't have missed it for the world, I am so proud to be your mum.

Anyone wishing to support the work of Meningitis Now you can make a donation to Calum's tribute fund.
http://meningitis-trust.tributefunds.com/fund/Calum+Sinclair+Macleod/showFund/

Foreword

As I wrote this book I knew that I wanted it to do many things one being to highlight the speed at which meningitis can strike and the devastation it can bring. I asked Sue Davie how she would describe it :-

"Meningitis is like a car crash – sudden, traumatic and life changing. And it is a thief – stealing the dreams parents have for their child; the ability for a grandfather to read to their deaf grandchild; the ability to earn money to look after your family; the confidence to go outside; life itself. At Meningitis Now (formed from the merger of Meningitis Trust and Meningitis UK, founders of the meningitis movement in the UK in the '80s), we meet families everyday facing a future changed forever. These people are our inspiration – fighting back against this dreadful disease, raising funds and awareness, and helping other people whose lives have been touched by meningitis.

Kim's book is honest and heartfelt and reflects her personal journey – a journey which, by sharing, she will undoubtedly help other families who have lost loved ones to meningitis or any other cause. I have no doubt that Calum would be immensely proud of the path that his mum has chosen to honour him."

Sue Davie

Chief Executive

Meningitis Trust/Meningitis UK

When you read the stories of kindness and compassion that we received there are some that stand out because we did not know these people but they meant a huge deal to Calum. I asked three most special people what was it that made them get in touch and take that extra step to help.

"It is a big regret that I never had the pleasure to meet Calum in person - Kim painted such a wonderful, fun, cheeky picture of him and I think we would have got on well. When I heard of his death I just had to call and see if there was anything I could do. I have kids of around the same age and meningitis is such a tangible threat for any of us that have children; their story broke my heart. But what a fantastic, courageous family - they are an inspiration."

Gino D'Acampo

"When I heard Calum's story, like everyone I was saddened and shocked. I was also moved and very proud that I was a part of something that brought him so much joy. Knowing that he was buried in his Fratellis T - shirt will stay with me forever.

I never had the chance to meet Calum but through the music we will always have a connection. "

Baz Fratelli

"Baz has summed up our connection with Calum. It was very hard to read of such pain and loss but I've just finished reading Kim's book and I really think she has done a great job of telling the story of her own and her family's journey out of such darkness. "

Jon Fratelli

The acts of kindness and compassion we received made such a difference to our lives. They also touched one of my favourite authors David R Hamilton, so much that he included some within his book Why Kindness is Good for You. I asked David what he thought of From Heartbreak to Happiness.

"Rarely do I come across a book that is so moving, inspiring and sings so loudly about the power of kindness and compassion to lift the human spirit and unite people in a common goal. This is such a book. I could not put it down from the moment I opened it"

David R Hamilton PhD

Action for Happiness is a great organisation, it exists to encourage each of us to take action to create a happier society. It was a real catalyst for me in acting on my ideas and has been a great source of support and resources for my happiness clubs. I was delighted when I was awarded a Happy Hero Award for UN International day of happiness. I asked Mark Williamson's what his thoughts were on the book.

"This is one of the most powerful and profoundly moving books I've ever read. Kim's story is heartbreaking but also deeply inspiring and full of hope and warmth. Rather to my surprise, despite the fact that I've read, talked about and tried out a huge range of happiness-boosting techniques, books and ideas - I feel the honesty and wisdom in her book has somehow left me better equipped to deal with adversity and loss. Her wisdom and honesty not only shows how we can each cope better with adversity, it also reaffirms the fundamental goodness of human nature and the amazing things that happen when we choose to live in a way that fosters happiness for ourselves and for others"

Mark Williamson PhD, MBA
Director, Action For Happiness

I hope that this book will lift your spirits and give you hope to live a happy life.

I would love to hear from you; to get in touch please email me at kim@stressthepositive.co.uk or visit my website:

www.stressthepositive.co.uk

Wishing you good health, love and happiness

Kim

x

Introduction

"Please no, anything but that. I can cope with anything but that." I had been wakened by the same nightmare for the third time in a month. I had this feeling that something terrible was going to happen to one of my children. I felt sick to my stomach as the panic gripped me; this was my worst nightmare. Or so I thought.

Five months later my worst nightmare came true when my wonderful son, Calum, contracted bacterial meningitis and died, aged 12 years and 10 months. I was plunged into a world of darkness and despair; a world where nothing made sense, where all my hopes and dreams had died with Calum.

However this is not a book full of despair and misery. It is a book filled with hope, for what I found was that I could cope. Not only cope, but thrive and be happy again.

I count myself lucky that in the years before Calum's death I had embarked on a journey of self-development, learning many valuable lessons, acquiring knowledge, skills and tools which had given me a strong foundation.

After losing Calum, I found myself on a journey that I had never planned. The road took me through the darkest of times, tested my beliefs and values, and gave me an insight into the workings of my mind and emotions. The journey through grief has been very difficult at times, but there have also been moments of great joy, laughter and happiness. I have been overwhelmed by the kindness of others, been inspired by some wonderful people, and been amazed at what can be achieved when you focus on something. It has brought me new friends and a total passion for spreading happiness to others.

I want to share my journey with you, to tell you the stories that lifted my heart and helped to heal the hole in it. This is more than a story; it is my roadmap out of despair and into happiness. I will share with you what I did to cope with my despair, what actions I took, what I said to myself, and what I thought along the way.

My wonderful happy son is no longer with me but I still feel connected to him and his love of life, and this has helped me to develop the life I now have. I believe that I honour my son by living my life well, by choosing to be happy and sharing that message with others.

All of us have a choice, maybe not about what happens, but certainly about how we react. Soon after Calum died, I made my choice to be happy again. I told family and friends that I would be, but in those early days I really didn't know how. It was as though I had forgotten what I knew; the shock and trauma wiped my memory for a time, but with the help of my friends and family I found my way and put my self-development knowledge to the test.

Six years on and I have been awarded a Happy Hero medal for the first International Day of Happiness. I am running Happiness Clubs, and have helped hundreds of people to add more happiness to their lives.

Whatever your reason for choosing this book, I truly believe that you can feel happier and create a more contented life. To do that, you have to try something new, think about things differently, and explore new opportunities along the way. I hope I can give you a route to follow, to give you some light, and to guide you to happier times.

If I can cope with every parent's worst nightmare and go on to lead a happy life, then you can improve your life too.

Part One

A Living Nightmare

Chapter One

"Mum, can I have some paracetamol? My head really hurts."

It is 3am on Wednesday, 10th October, 2007 and I wake to find my son, Calum, standing next to our bed. I get up and give him the tablets. Fifteen minutes later he is saying it is very sore, so I give him ibuprofen and reassure him the pain will go away as I put a cold compress on his head.

When he starts to cry with the pain, I call NHS 24. "Has he got a rash? Is his neck stiff and sore? Does he avoid bright light?" the woman asks. No is the response to all her questions, but she can hear him crying and tells me to take him to the out-of-hours emergency GP service.

I wake my husband, Sinclair. "I need to take Calum to Stobhill" I tell him. "He has a really bad headache. You stay here with Kirsten." Sinclair gives Calum a sympathetic cuddle as he helps him into his jacket. "See you soon, pal."

I drive Calum the two miles to our local hospital with a knot in my stomach. He is getting more upset and agitated as we drive into the hospital grounds. "Mum, I can't feel my hands and feet," he cries. Panic grips me as I abandon the car outside the entrance to the GP service, and try to help Calum out of the passenger's seat.

He collapses on the pavement, unable to walk, so I run frantically into the reception area to ask for help. Someone appears with a wheelchair and whisks Calum straight in to see the GP.

The doctor examines him, takes his temperature and asks me questions. "Calum had flu-like symptoms earlier in the day," I explain. "He saw our family GP, but she thought it was a return of a throat infection he had a couple of weeks ago. He seemed okay, ate his dinner and watched a movie before bed." "I think he could have meningitis," the emergency doctor tells me, giving Calum two shots of antibiotics. "You need to take him to Yorkhill Hospital. Have you got a car? Can you take him, or do you need to wait for the patient transport service?"

My head is spinning, my heart is pounding. This is serious. "I'll take him NOW!" I rush my son out of the door and into the car. I need to let Sinclair know, but the battery on my mobile phone has died. No time; just drive.

The journey to Yorkhill Children's Hospital is only about four miles but it seems like a lifetime as I try to calm my brain and concentrate. What is the quickest route there? Calum is screaming with the pain and panicking beside me. "Help me, Mum, please help me," he screams over and over as I try to comfort him and drive.

I reach the entrance to the hospital just as Calum is sick, throwing up all over himself and the car. I bring the car to a screeching halt outside Accident and Emergency, jump out and run screaming into the hospital. "Please help me, my son needs help. I've come from Stobhill. They think he has meningitis."

A nurse follows me out to the car and helps Calum into a wheelchair. "Why are you not in an ambulance?" he shouts. I start to explain but he is already rushing Calum, now semi-conscious, into the emergency room.

I hand the letter the GP gave me to the receptionist, impatiently answer her questions, then follow Calum into the emergency room. It is chaos. Doctors and nurses rush around attaching wires and tubes to my little boy. "How long has he been like this? Could he have taken any drugs?" they ask. Drugs? Of course not, my gorgeous son is only 12!

Calum is writhing in pain, covered in sick and very confused. I try to calm him as the doctors work on him. His blood pressure, heart rate and temperature are very erratic. I can see they are worried. "We need to sedate him and put him on a ventilator. He is dangerously ill and we are not sure what it is," I am told.

"Do it, please help him," I plead as the panic and fear grips me. I feel faint, sick and disconnected. This can't be happening.

"It could be meningitis or some other virus or infection; it could be something on his brain. So we need to get a scan now."

The nurse leads me to a small waiting room. I need to call Sinclair; he doesn't even know we are here. The phone answers straight away. "You need to come to Yorkhill. It's serious, they think Calum has meningitis," I blurt out.

"What? Where? Oh my God, what about Kirsten?" I can hear the shock and worry in his voice.

"I'll phone Robert and Jane, and get them," I tell him. Robert is Sinclair's cousin and his wife, Jane had been our childminder, looking after both Calum and his wee sister, Kirsten, since they were babies. I look at my watch: 6.20am. If the phone rings at this hour, you know something's wrong.

The minute Robert answers, I take a deep breath. "Calum's in Yorkhill, it's serious, they think it's meningitis." The words are rushing out. "Please can you bring Sinclair here, and can Jane stay with Kirsten?"

"What? Yes. Where?"

And so begins the day that will change so many lives forever.

I sit in the waiting room on my own. Three-and-a-half hours ago, I was asleep – how can this be happening? I am shaking, scared and full of panic as I wait desperately for Sinclair. He arrives with Robert within 30 minutes of my call. "Where is Calum? What's happening?"

We sit together waiting for news, while the nurses kindly offer tea and toast. How can I possibly eat? I feel sick with worry.

A doctor appears. "Calum has had the scan and is being taken to Intensive Care. We don't know what it is yet. It is very serious, but the good news is there is no inflammation on his brain."

Okay, I tell myself, that's good news. Come on, Calum, please get better.

We are taken to the Intensive Care Unit and sit in another waiting room. I notice leaflets about meningitis, and my eyes are drawn to some information about organ donation. No, ignore that. He will be fine, he's going to be okay. I keep that thought running around my head.

It's now 8.30 am and we need to let our families know. More shocked phone calls, I apologise as I break the news, as though I am responsible for upsetting their lives.

"We are on our way, we'll be there as soon as we can," my mum tells me.

Jane arrives first, having taken Kirsten to school. She is only eight and adores her big brother. I know she will be worried, but at least she has some distractions for now.

It seems like an age before we can see Calum. We are taken into the ICU, to a room where he is lying on a bed surrounded by machines. He has tubes and wires everywhere. The machines bleep and make unusual noises as they monitor his every function and keep him alive.

Sinclair and I cling to each other. Oh, my boy. I touch his hand and his hair, he looks like he is sleeping. "We're here, Calum, Mum and Dad are here." I tell him. "We love you. Don't worry, you will be okay." But my heart is filled with fear and worry, Sinclair and I both cry as we leave the room.

For the rest of the day, people come to support us. The family room is soon filled and, with each new arrival, I answer their questions; the shock is evident on their faces. That same shock has me on auto-pilot. I am walking and talking, but I feel disconnected from my body at times.

Jane collects Kirsten from school and brings her to the hospital. My poor baby girl is so scared. "Will Calum be okay?" she asks.

"We hope so," I reply, trying to reassure her. But she doesn't look well. She has a bit of a temperature and I ask the doctor if they can check her over, too. "Take her down to A&E," they say.

So here I am, 7.30pm back in A&E with Kirsten. My heart is pounding again, I breathe slowly to keep calm for her.

"We don't know what she has, but she is brewing some infection so we need to take some blood," the doctor says. Kirsten reacts calmly but my heart skips a beat. Then the news comes: "We want to admit her overnight, she could have meningitis so we want to give her some intravenous antibiotics and keep a close eye on her. Just in case!"

No, please, not both of them. I am screaming inside my head as I smile at Kirsten and reassure her she is okay. Jane agrees to stay in the room with Kirsten overnight.

More family and friends arrive to see Calum. I tell everyone – no crying at his bedside, talk to him about anything positive, you don't know what he can hear. Tell him he can fight this, tell him he'll be okay.

We take it in turns to spend time with him, crying when we leave his room and clinging to each other for comfort and strength. We talk to him about his friends, his computer games, read to him. We arrange for a CD player and play his favourite band, the Fratellis, for him. We take it in turns all night, as I go between my two precious children – Calum in the ICU, and Kirsten in the room on a ward upstairs.

The next day brings good news for Kirsten; she doesn't have meningitis and can go home. But we still don't know about Calum. There is no change, he is still gravely ill and the wonderful ICU nurses are keeping him as comfortable as possible while they adjust the mix of medicines, fluids and oxygen.

"We need to do an MRI scan and a lumbar puncture. Your son is seriously ill and this is dangerous, but we need to confirm what we are dealing with," the doctors tell us.

More anxious waiting, phone calls to update people. My mum, stepdad and sister are still with us, so we all need some clean clothes and a wash. Others arrange this, food appears, and somehow the time passes. We have camped out in this family room, it's become our place, filled with support and love. Friends and family from near and far all stop what they are doing and come to us. Many don't know what to do or say, but a hug is all that is needed.

Then comes the news we have dreaded. The doctors take Sinclair and me into a small interview room and explain that Calum has bacterial meningitis. It has attacked his brain stem and there is nothing that they can do. His brain is dead; it is only the machines that are keeping him alive.

"NO, NO! You must be wrong, surely there is something you can do? Calum was fit and healthy, how can he be dead? PLEASE!" I plead. But there is nothing that can save him.

"He could help save others. Would you consider organ donation?" they ask. "Will you think about it?"

My world comes crashing down. This can't be true – Sinclair and I have two wonderful children and a good life. This isn't in my plan for us.

We have to tell our family in the room across the hall. More tears and questions. "Why him? Take me instead," says my mum. "I have had my life; his is only beginning." We all sob and wail together.

Next comes the hardest thing I have ever done. I have to tell my daughter that her big brother isn't coming home. The boy she loves so much, the one who plays with her and shares everything with her, with such love and kindness. is no longer going to be with her. Somehow I find the words, I hold her and answer her questions. But there is no answer to "Why Calum?"Back to the hospital. We have to answer the question of organ donation. I have carried a donor card for years, but now they are asking for my son's organs. He just looks as if he is sleeping. How can I let them cut into him? But the meningitis bacteria went straight to his brain – nothing else has been affected.

Sinclair and I talk about Calum, how he helped everyone, how he cared for others; we think about what he would do. We also sit and talk about other parents who are sitting by their child's bed, hoping and praying that someone can save their youngster. Calum could do this, he could give them hope and maybe save lives.

There is no hope for us, but some good could come for others. Yes, we say, go ahead.

And so the organ transplant teams spring into action. We get to meet a co-ordinator who talks us through it all. "You can have anything except his eyes," I tell them. "Don't touch his beautiful blue eyes." So we sign the forms and then the longest night of our lives begins.

The doctors need to perform two tests to ensure that there is no brain activity. This involves taking the drugs out of Calum's system overnight and doing the tests the next day. So we all stay another night in the hospital, talking and reading to Calum, playing his music, stroking his hair, holding his hand.

But this night we have no hope. This night we know it will be the last we will ever spend with him. This really is the dark night of the soul. We call family and friends and tell them to come if they want to say goodbye.

Calum is so loved. The nurses comment on how many "aunties" he has, how he has touched so many lives and is clearly a very special young man.

The nurses continue to care for him – and us – with such warmth and understanding. They really are angels. I don't know how they do that job every day, with such compassion and love yet facing the worst times imaginable for so many families.

And so the time finally comes to leave my beloved son; to say goodbye to him. I remember Calum at about three years old, telling me he would never leave me, he was going to stay with me forever.

This is all wrong. I was leaving Calum, it's not right. But Sinclair pulls me away. Calum has gone – this is only his shell and we have to let the transplant team do their job.

I sit quietly in the car on the way home. I look at the world carrying on as normal. People are walking and talking, going shopping, making dinner, laughing. How is that possible? Don't they know everything has changed? Don't they know that the world is different?

The lights have gone out in my world. It is Friday, 12th October, 2007 and my wonderful, handsome, happy, smiling boy is dead.

Chapter 2

I wake up. It's Saturday morning and, for just a second, it's a normal day. Then my eyes open and the harsh reality floods in. Life will never be normal again; Calum is dead.

It's hard to describe the shock; it's a bit like I am tuned to a different frequency to the world. I can see and hear what is going on, but I don't feel connected.

The house smells of lillies, and I don't have enough vases for the flowers that are here already. Friends appear carrying bags full of shopping, looking for a way to feel helpful, searching for some way to ease our pain. And so the procession of visitors, cups of tea, cards, flowers, tears and storytelling begins.

"What happened?" they ask. I must tell the story hundreds of times, but I need to tell it, as if by doing so I am convincing myself that it is real. I find myself apologising as I see others cry.

I need to see Calum. I left him still breathing in the hospital. I need to see him; is he really dead? I phone Yorkhill and am told a nurse will take me to see him in the Chapel of Rest. My mum, sister and Jane all come with me.

I go into the room on my own. It is very cold, and Calum is lying on a bed covered with a blanket. He looks peaceful but I can see his spirit has gone. He is so cold to my touch, I want to warm him up. "I love you, I am so sorry, Calum," I whisper. "I brought you some of your things". It seems a bit strange that I have brought him some toy cars and a Dr Who audio book, but it feels really important for him to have some of his things.

I spend some time talking to my boy. "You need to let us know that you are okay," I plead. "Please." I need to know that his spirit is still around somehow, I need to know he is cared for, I am worried he will be alone.

Mum, Lynda and Jane all spend time with Calum, then it is time to go. I feel calmer now that I have seen him, but I also feel as though he is with me. In the car we talk about Calum and how he loved to laugh. I recall a recent lunch with Mum and Lynda, when we were all laughing and playing some game but I can't remember what it was all about.

Mum and Lynda give each other a strange look. "We were laughing about inappropriate songs to play at funerals," Lynda explains. I laugh, "Oh yes, now I remember." Calum won the contest with *Staying Alive* by the Bee Gees.

We arrive back home. Sinclair asks how I am and apologises for not coming. He couldn't face it. "It was better than I thought," I say. Others are asking questions when I suddenly hear the song that is playing – *Staying Alive* by the Bee

Gees. With over 10,000 songs on random play on the iTunes list, this stops me in my tracks.

"Listen!" I shout over the chatter. Lynda, Jane and my mum all look at me as I smile and explain, "Calum just let us know he is okay."

Reflections

The speed at which meningitis can strike is scary. The shock and trauma of Calum's death was nothing like I had ever experienced. Even though we had lived through tragedy and death of loved ones before, nothing prepared me for it.

I clung on to little things that seemed so important – like taking Calum toy cars. It was as though my brain could only process small things. I remember standing by the kettle and trying to think how to make tea.

But I did not fall apart, I continued to function. I was more worried about Kirsten and Sinclair, how would they cope? What could I do to help them? A friend gave us a candle. "To bring a little light in the darkness," she said.

That candle became so important to me. I kept a candle burning every hour I was awake. I looked at the flame, and maybe it did provide a little light in my darkness. There were practical things to be done. My son's funeral to arrange.

Words of Hope

Find your light in the darkness. It may be the smallest of lights but it can give you something to cling to.

Chapter 3

How do we begin to organise a funeral for Calum? It's Monday. Last Monday, everything was normal; now we are talking about burying our son. The one thing I know for certain – it won't be a religious service and I won't wear black.

We decide on a Humanist service and are put it touch with a wonderful lady. Linda comes to discuss Calum with us, to hear about his life, the stories, and all that he was. It is so good to talk about Calum, to tell her how wonderful he was, how he adored his sister, how he had so many friends, what he liked and disliked, what he believed in and hoped for. How loved he was. It seems strange to say it is a good experience, but it lifts our spirits as we laugh at the stories and happy memories and tell of our pride in our son. Linda helps us to make his funeral a celebration of his life.

It is difficult to find a venue to hold the service. We want to stay close and know we need a large space for everyone that will come. The council-run hall is being used the morning we want to have the service; I am so stressed while waiting to hear if it can happen there.

We organise family, friends and teachers to talk, and share their memories. I want to shield my daughter, nieces and Calum's friends from the pain and hurt of the funeral. I don't want them to face his coffin, as if this will somehow make it easier, so we will cover the coffin with the Scotland flag and arrange to place it at the side of the room.

We dress him in his favourite T-shirt, one that says 'Mon The Fratellis' and place in his coffin drawings from Kirsten and our niece Isla, photographs of our family, CDs of The Fratellis and a Star Wars toy.

Funerals are always sad but burying your child is not the natural order of things. I am so grateful to all the wonderful people who come to hear about Calum and to support us. I have been to many funerals over the years, some cold and almost unfeeling, and others very personal and full of love. I want everyone to leave knowing more about how wonderful Calum was, how funny he was, to hear how loved he was, and to see what a bright light he has been on this earth.

We play his favourite music and sing, *You've Got a Friend In Me* – the Toy Story theme tune – as this was one of his favourite movies and the words just so capture him. Then *500 Miles*, by The Proclaimers.

I am holding Kirsten in my arms and singing at the top of my voice as I celebrate my son's life. The stories and memories shared by others make my heart swell with pride. Calum was loved by so many people.

His coffin is carried out of the hall to *Chelsea Dagger* by The Fratellis, the song he had been learning to play on his guitar. I am sure he would have approved.

Calum's burial is accompanied by a lament on the bagpipes. I watch as they lower my son's body into the ground; it is almost surreal. We have just been laughing and sharing stories of my happy, caring, lovable boy, I don't want to put him in that cold and dark place.

I look around at the faces of family and friends, etched with pain and tears. We all need each other, we need to support and help each other; we have all lost Calum.

Reflections

Looking back on Calum's funeral, I am proud of the send-off he got. So many people have spoken to us over the years, saying that it was one of the saddest but most uplifting funerals they have ever attended. I realise, though, that I could not shield the children from the hard realities of death. Many children have to come to terms with the death of a grandparent, parent, sibling or friend. We all have to face the truth that death is a part of life, and trying to protect them could mean delaying that reality being accepted.

Words of hope

Even in the bleakest times, talking about our loved ones can lift our hearts. Maybe only for a minute, but a minute of joy is one less of despair.

Chapter 4

What now? The funeral is over, so what do we do? What is my life now? People continue to come to see us, cards and letters from hundreds of people (some we don't even know) line the room, more flowers appear, cakes, pots of soup, teddies for Kirsten. I appreciate them all; the kindness surrounds me like a warm blanket.

But our house is too quiet. This doesn't feel like home – where are the boys? Where is the constant troupe of kids laughing, playing music and computer games? There's no-one to ask, "How many am I feeding tonight?" Calum isn't saying, can Garry/Marcus/Gavin, etc, stay over tonight? So it's not only Calum that I have lost, but the fun and energy of his friends too.

Calum's friends are also lost – they are missing him and want to do something. They all come and visit us. It takes a lot of courage, I reckon, for 12/13-year-old boys to come in to see how we are. They spend time in his room, play with Kirsten and take our dog out. They are a special bunch indeed. But they want to do more – they want to do something in Calum's memory. To raise some money for charity. And so our fundraising efforts begin.

Together we decide that we will celebrate Calum's 13th birthday – it is about six weeks away on 8th December, 2007. The ideas come thick and fast from this group of kids: sponsored gaming sessions, football, raffles, an auction. They all want to do it and get the school involved, to raise a lot of money for meningitis charities. They need to do it.

So once a week for the next six weeks our house is filled with the buzz and excitement of a growing group of Calum's friends and a very special teacher, David Hepburn. (David was Calum's registration and history teacher. He was very upset by Calum's death and sent us a beautiful letter telling us how wonderful our son was, how helpful and kind he was. I will treasure this forever.)

The plans grow more ambitious each week, but I love it. For one night I live my old life; I can almost hear Calum shouting excitedly amongst them, cheering and laughing with them. It is suggested that an auction could raise a lot of money. How about we contact all the people that Calum really loved – musicians and bands, DJs, celebrities, the TV programmes he watched, the football teams, the actors, books and films he loved – and ask if they can donate an item for the auction? So the list is drawn up – The Fratellis, Biffy Clyro, Kasabian, The Proclaimers, Amy McDonald, Dominik Diamond from XFM, his favourite chefs Gino

D'Acampo and Nigella Lawson, David Tennant, Peter Kay, Stephen Fry, JK Rowling, Ewan McGregor are just a few!

This list is not just a random list of celebs, it is a list of people who added something to Calum's life. I so want these people to know about my son and how they inspired, entertained and enhanced his life. So we start to contact them, and I am amazed by the generosity that we receive – books, T-shirts, merchandise, CDs, a guitar, signed photos all come flooding in.

There are some on the list that I really want to connect with. The ones that I know had an extra special place in Calum's heart: The Fratellis and Gino D'Acampo, the Italian chef.

I send letters out, contact agents and fan sites in my quest. The boys all help, using Facebook and all the connections they can. The auction items are increasing, alongside the plans for sponsored gaming sessions, tombola, football, games, food, music. It is all becoming a bit overwhelming at times; trying to temper the boys' enthusiasm is like wrestling cats!

Their school – Bishopbriggs Academy – has a wonderful set of teachers, led by an excellent Head Teacher, Gordon Moulsdale. They are keen to do anything they can to help make this day a success, to give the pupils, teachers and the whole community the opportunity to do something to honour Calum.

They are also very sensitive to our needs and I will be forever grateful to Gordon Moulsdale, Moira Carberry

(Calum's year head) David Hepburn, and the rest of the teaching staff, for taking on this challenge.

One night in November my phone rings. "Hello, is that Kim?" I hear an Italian accent. "It's Gino – Gino D'Acampo. I am so sorry for the loss of your son. How can I help you?"

Wow – I am bowled over, Gino has actually called me!

Some years later, Kim & Kirsten met Gino to say thanks

I tell him how much he meant to Calum, how he loved to watch *Ready Steady Cook* to see if Gino was on, and would get really excited about it. How he had started to cook, and loved Gino's energy and sense of fun.

"You helped create some wonderful memories for us," I tell him.

Gino is so warm, caring and genuine, asking how we are coping and offers to send books.

46

That phone call has such an impact on me, and on our family. Calum adored him and now Gino knew about Calum. The fact that he has made the effort to phone me himself is huge; he doesn't know us, but this act of kindness really lifts me.

The big day is getting closer – many friends and family offer to help, more and more donations arrive. People we don't know are donating prized possessions for our auction. The school are busy co-ordinating lots of activities, food and publicity. We are energised by everything, but exhausted by it too. There are times when I feel that this is too much. What have we done? How can we do all of this? Then I meet friends who ask how they can help and it becomes manageable again.

The group of friends meeting at our house grows too, as others get involved to help. The big objective is to get to The Fratellis. All our attention is on this – Calum loved music. He had a large iTunes collection and had started going to gigs with us. The Fratellis had really captured him – they inspired him to learn the guitar, *Chelsea Dagger* was the last song he was learning, and of course he was buried in his Fratellis T-shirt. I want them to know all this, even more than I want anything from them.

The kids post notes on their website, via the fan pages, and any way they can think of, but nothing seems to be getting to the band. Then I get a call from my friend Elaine. She tells me how she has just found out that she works beside Baz's (bass player) sister! Not only that, but after she told her the story, she called her brother – and the band wants to meet me!

Friday, 7th December, 2007, I park outside the studios of my son's heroes. I tell myself to hold it together as I go inside to meet Baz, Jon and Mince. They are so lovely; they apologise for the difficulty in getting to them and ask about Calum. I tell them all about my wonderful son, his plans to have a band with his pals, learning the guitar and loving

Fratellis' treasures

their music. I thank them for the wonderful memory I have of being with him at their gig and tell them the awful tale of his death.

Their genuine compassion is extremely touching and their generosity blows me away. They present me with the original canvas artwork for *Chelsea Dagger*, a Fratelli's drum skin, and then Jon hands me his cream Fender guitar that he played *Chelsea Dagger* on. I am rarely speechless, but this is one of those moments; I am completely overwhelmed.

I thank them so much, give them a photo of Calum, and explain that I had better get back to the chaos of preparation for the next day. The guys suggest I bring Calum's friends to

Meeting the Fratellis during a studio visit

the studios to meet them some time, and help me out to the car with my treasures.

But where is my car? No, this can't be happening! I look frantically around for it; I am sure I parked it there. Has it been stolen? Baz looks at the space where I left it, just on the edge of a bus stop. "There's no glass, so maybe it got lifted by traffic wardens," he suggests.

That's it! The floodgates open and I just stand there sobbing. What can I do?

The guys are fabulous – they lead me back inside. "Don't worry, we'll sort it," they say. Baz makes some phone calls, Jon gives me a hug, and Mince makes me tea. Within a few minutes they establish my car is heading to the pound, organise their chauffeur to collect me and take me to the car, and arrange to pay the fine. Wow! Not only fantastic musicians but wonderful human beings.

I get home some time later with an unbelievable story of kindness and generosity that I know will be shared many times.

The next day is Calum's 13th birthday and it is the biggest birthday party he ever had! Over 800 people turn up to the school fundraising day. We raise over £6,600 on the day and we haven't even auctioned the Fratellis' gifts (we would raise more cash with them the following year).

The energy, enthusiasm, compassion, courage and kindness of everyone taking part is huge. It is a tough day for us too, but what a way to celebrate Calum's birthday. I think it helps so many of his friends, teachers and our family.

Reflections

It is amazing how an idea can build into such a heart-warming event. I often think of the energy that this created, of the wonder that the two who were so important to Calum on that list were the two that I had direct contact with – Gino D'Acampo and The Fratellis. When people come together with a shared objective, it is wonderful what can be achieved. The stories really gave everyone such a boost, but it wasn't really the stories, it was the acts of kindness and compassion for another human being that made such a difference. Some of those acts of kindness were more unusual because of the celebrities concerned, but everyone who wrote, cooked, baked cakes, gave flowers, cleaned, volunteered, donated items or their time, had an impact on us. Tragedy and difficult times can bring out the best in people.

Words of hope

Put your thoughts out there; if you need help, ask. If you can help someone else, do it. We can all benefit by helping someone in whatever way we can.

Part Two

Life Goes On

Chapter 5

I understand now why people get so passionate about fundraising for a charity which is connected with a loved one. We set up a tribute fund in Calum's name at the Meningitis Trust and this galvanised our family and friends to take action. They ran 10k races, marathons, climbed mountains, organised sponsored events and sold books. It was as if we were honouring Calum not by the amount of money raised but by the actions we took. That first event had been so rewarding, uplifting and encouraging, but the emotional crash afterwards was equally hard. Now I was back to the harsh reality of life, trying to find some new normal.

Not long after Calum died, I started to write to him. I had this real desire to be connected to him and, at the same time, a real fear that he would drift further from me. Writing was a way to keep him close.

I poured out my heart in those journal letters; I still write to him now. Some pages are smeared with my tears, as I told him how much I loved and missed him, how angry I felt, or the despair that overwhelmed me that day. I often wrote at night when I couldn't sleep – there was no point in lying in bed, so I would go downstairs and pour all my thoughts onto paper. The combination of dumping my thoughts, letting go of the tears, and physically writing, certainly helped me.

I could be honest and say the things that were in my head. No-one read the letters to Calum, only me. I would tell him about our lives, too, and what was happening – almost as though he was away on holiday. I did know that he wasn't coming home, but it still hadn't sunk in that this was forever.

I went to visit my GP, who is a very wise and kind man. Even though his surgery was busy, he spent a lot of time with me, listening to me talk about my sense of loss. He gave me some really good advice that I have shared with many people:

- Don't bottle up your emotions; let them out. Scream, shout, cry – whatever you need to.
- There are two questions that will drive you mad, so don't ask them. Why Calum? And, What if..?
- Be honest with others, ask for help and let people help.

He explained that although I didn't want to hear the "time will make it better" statement, it was true. He reassured me that I could cope and that life would improve, but it would be a rocky road. And he didn't offer me medication or counselling, because he knew that grief is a natural and necessary process. In today's society we often want the quick fix, a tablet to take away the pain. Dealing with the death of a loved one, and particularly a child, can not be healed with a tablet.

I did follow his advice. I cried into Calum's t-shirt, sometimes with huge wracking sobs that seemed to go on for hours. I let it flow. I can remember thinking that the tears would never end, but they did and I felt better after them. I would also go into the field a mile or so from our house and scream at the top of my voice. I am amazed that the police never arrived to see who was being murdered!

The questions to avoid are so important. I knew why my doctor told me this. There were no answers, so all this would do would be to drive me in a negative cycle of despair. The questions did appear in my thoughts at times, but I would consciously choose to focus on something else.

Being honest about how I felt was not always easy, but some family and friends truly wanted to know. If you are lucky enough to have people like this in your life, then you are blessed. I didn't have to pretend or even speak; they would call and offer help, and I accepted.

Sinclair and I agreed from the day that Calum died that we needed to be honest with each other about how we were feeling. We both knew that many marriages don't survive the death of a child. We seemed to be in an ebb and flow of emotion – when I was really low, Sinclair would be stronger. He would cuddle me, let me cry or talk, and handle the practical things. When Sinclair dipped, I would be the strong one and I would encourage him to talk about how he felt. It was harder for him to put into words how deep his grief was. I could see his emotional pain transform into physical pain as his back went into spasms and his stomach caused him pain and eating problems.

I describe these early days as black and bleak. It was as if the colour had drained from my life. The loss of motivation and zest for life felt overwhelming at times. There were days when I struggled to get out of bed. Kirsten had drawn me a picture of a colourful rainbow, so I pinned it beside my bed. I would look at that picture and think of her, of how much she needed me and how much I needed her too. I would think of the happier times that we had spent as a family, reliving those happy memories in my head, drawing energy and love from them. This would be enough to get me up; a start for the day.

I developed lots of little boosters that helped me through those black days. I have a few positive quote books – one of my favourites then was "1001 Things to Make You Smile" by Marion Kaplinsky, which is full of little stories, jokes and sayings, and I would read a few pages until I did smile.

I would use different aromatherapy oils to boost my mood. I wore them like perfume on my clothes and would go between bergamot, peppermint and lavender. I would often be found sniffing my cardigan!

I am lucky to have a dog, Bracken; a beautiful Shetland collie. He needed to get out, so I had no option but to go out for a walk. Getting moving helped to lift me, although there were many walks where I had tears running down my cheeks too. Bracken always sensed how I was feeling; if I was crying, he would lick my face to wash away the tears. Animals are very aware of our emotional state, and he seemed to want to comfort me.

Looking up to the sky is another simple pick-me-up I used. It lifts you out of your emotions and into your visual area. Such a simple idea, but it really can give you a lift of mood.

Some days I just needed to wrap myself up and watch some TV, something to distract me from my thoughts if I was really low on energy.

The one constant factor was that I talked to Calum, sometimes out loud, other times in my head. I would ask for his help when I was struggling, or ask him to let me know how he was. I so wanted to feel that connection with him. I wanted more signs that he was okay.

Gradually the days became a little less bleak, more grey than black, then ever so gently the colour began to appear. I started to feel a little more energetic.

I wrote the following in a letter to Calum on the 21st January, 2008. "I know that you want to see me smile and be the happy mum you loved. I will do it for you and for Kirsten. I will also do it for me and your dad. I will use this in my work and help others to heal their pain."

Reflections

In those early days, I was overwhelmed by the depth of my emotions. If you are scared that you will disappear into the void never to return, then have hope. Little things make a difference; one thought or memory can connect with positive feelings enough to give you a boost.

Your brain does not know the difference between something that is actually happening now or something you are imagining. Your body will react as if it's happening, so if you can remember some happy memories this may make the difference between having a black day to a grey one.

Finding simple things to help me smile and feel happier did not take Calum's loss away, but it helped me to cope better with it. These simple strategies allowed me to look after Kirsten and Sinclair, and started the healing process, supporting me in my grief.

Words of Hope

Simple things can make a difference. Aromatherapy oils, quote books and happy memories can help you through tough days.

Chapter 6

We had passed Calum's birthday in December, but now we faced Christmas. How could we have Christmas? It had always been a very special time for our family, filled with our own traditions, fun and lots of laughter, so I really could not see a way for us to celebrate this so soon.

Everywhere I went I was faced with Christmas carols, happy smiling images of families having fun around their festive trees and enjoying dinner together. I really wanted to scream and run. And yet I had Kirsten to consider. She was only eight and deserved the best Christmas that we could give her.

I decided not to write Christmas cards; I couldn't face only writing three names instead of four. It was just too soon, but I figured that family and friends would forgive us. (Now whenever I write a card to anyone and put our three names, I always add four kisses on it. It is my way of including Calum, too.)

The run-up to that first Christmas was hard, our extended family was unsure of what to do and how to help. I accepted the practical help to buy gifts for Kirsten and my nieces. I had no energy to think about presents.

We asked my family to spend the day with us to make it as normal as possible for Kirsten and to share the load. The only difference was that I didn't want to have a sit-down Christmas dinner. I couldn't face sitting around the table without Calum there. Everyone agreed and surprisingly, our first Christmas Day without Calum was okay. It was different, of course, but many friends and family made the effort to visit or call us. We had a house full of people in the evening, and played a quiz. The laughter and fun really helped to lift our spirits.

New Year was a very different story. Traditionally in Scotland, Hogmanay is celebrated with family and friends, sharing food and drink at "the bells" to see out the old year and in with the new. On the 31st December 2007, I became overwhelmed by the dread of the next year approaching. I was faced with a full year without Calum, and I didn't want to do it. There would be no planning for happy times together, no holidays, no fun with all Calum's friends.

I remembered the previous New Year, when everything had been exciting as I was just starting my new business, Stress the Positive. My plans to help people struggling with depression, stress and anxiety to find happier times, now seemed far away as I fought the tears and feeling of doom.

Our family and friends came to our rescue again, supplying us with food, and looking after Kirsten to give us space and let us grieve. Within a day or two I began to feel a bit better, the dark clouds moved slightly and I even started to think about the year ahead. I began to make plans to buy a caravan in St Andrews.

There are lots of firsts to be dealt with after a death. From the first time that you go out without the person, through to big occasions like Christmas, Easter and birthdays. My next big challenge was to be Mother's Day.

Mother's Day – a day to celebrate and thank your mum for all that she does for you. I wanted Calum back more than anything. "I am your mum and you should be here," I wrote in my journal. The ache in my heart was so sore. Heartache through grief is a physical pain. My heart really did feel like there was a hole in it.

I knew that I needed some help to heal it, to let go of some of the fear, guilt and anger at Calum not being here. My knowledge of Neuro Linguistic Programming (NLP) was reconnecting. I had used some techniques to let go of the trauma of the dash to hospital, so that I could now drive the car without reliving that nightmare. But I knew that I needed some help to move forwards with my life.

I turned to a trusted friend and fellow NLP professional, Liesha, and she was just the tonic I needed. She helped me to let go of the guilt I held onto for not saving Calum, and for wanting to feel better! Whoever said that emotions follow a logical route? She also helped me to create some light to look towards the future with a bit of hope for a better life.

Together we planted seeds in my future timeline to grow and nurture, to provide a gentle route for a way back to working with others. To find a way to make something meaningful of this tragedy. I knew I was learning some really important life lessons and that this must be used to help give others hope.

Family birthdays and celebrations were still a difficult experience for us. I am a people person and love a gathering. But it was a struggle to attend things – dinners and parties meant that we went without Calum. It was tough, but we went. I knew that Calum would not want us to stay home. The dread of the days leading up to anniversaries, parties or events, would disappear on the day. I can honestly say that we often really enjoyed those nights, and I am glad that we pushed through the pain barrier.

The Easter school holidays approached. We had bought a caravan in St Andrews, but it wasn't ready yet. We decided to rent a house nearby and go away for a few days with Sinclair's sister and family. I had always loved holidays, the planning for days out, picnics and fun. Part of me craved that normality as I found myself imagining some fun times, but I was also struck with the terrible sense of loss that Calum would not be with us.

On the Saturday we were due to leave, I woke up crying. I didn't want to go without him. I went to Calum's grave and left a toy car, telling him I would bring him back a seashell. But I also knew that I needed to go – I needed to create new memories for us all. I did take his framed photo with us, so that he didn't seem too far away.

The summer holidays were a real mix of emotions. We filled our time at our new caravan. The sea is so calming and St Andrews holds such dear memories for us. But it was still a first – the first summer without Calum. There were dark days, even in the sunshine; days where my motivation was low. I was angry that Calum was not there. It wasn't fair he wasn't asking his usual question: "Where are we going tomorrow, Mum?"

Having friends join us really helped. The diversion of energy took me out of my low mood and engaged me in laughter.

August 29th 2008 was my first birthday without Calum. I woke feeling sad; I so wanted to have him near me. I spoke to him in my head, asking him to come close and let me know he was okay. Later that day, I took Bracken for a walk in the park. As I stood watching him sniff around the trees, I noticed a large butterfly coming towards me. It circled around my head then flew down towards my foot and settled on my shoe. It stretched out its wings and unveiled these beautiful "blue eyes" on its wings. I was amazed; I had never seen a butterfly like it.

I reached into my pocket and got out my phone. The butterfly stayed calm on my foot as I took photos of it. I was rooted to the spot as it sat there for almost five minutes, then flew off. My heart felt like it was bursting full of love; I have never felt an experience like it. I said thank you to Calum for my birthday gift. His beautiful blue eyes had shone out to me through a butterfly.

A birthday gift'

Reflections

The first year after a death is a year of finding your feet, just like a baby begins to crawl, pulls itself up and holds on to others' hands for stability. You, too, can learn to walk again. Expect to fall down occasionally, bump your head, and scrape your knees, but know that your desire to walk will take over. Accept the help of those who offer their hand along the way.

The butterfly is such a symbol of hope and transformation. Many people have told tales of seeing butterflies after a loved one has died. I chose to see this as a present from Calum, of further proof that he had transformed into another energy; one that could not be seen, but one that could hear and connect with me on some level. That belief helped me to thrive.

You may have different beliefs. What is a belief? It is only a thought that we have decided is true. Beliefs can be challenged and questioned and changed.

Words of hope

Find meaning and connection with our loved ones through nature. Look out for your own messages.

Chapter 7

Grief has many stages: shock, disbelief, anger, despair, healing, and finally, acceptance. From my experience, is it not a linear process. I found myself jumping back and forwards through the thoughts and emotions. As we headed towards the first anniversary of Calum's death, I had experienced almost all of them – acceptance was still to come.

That first year without my son had taken its toll on me, our family and friends. We had all had difficult times, emotionally and physically. I was learning to live without Calum, but I didn't like it.

The hardest part for me was watching my daughter and trying to help her. She was so lost at times, scared by the world that could rob her of her big brother and best friend in the blink of an eye. The nightmares of being abandoned did not only affect her sleep, she was scared to let me out of her sight for a long time. Separation anxiety initially made going to school or to a friend's house hard. Thankfully, I had a good relationship with her school, and together we developed a plan of action. Short times in school to begin with, me staying in the building for a while, giving her a physical thing to hold of mine, and creating a space for her to go if it all got too much. We built up the time in school gradually until she felt safe again.

But I also had to help her adjust to Calum not coming home. She did not want to face the reality of his death. I so wanted to protect her and take away this pain; it was a double hurt. I hurt from the loss of my son and I hurt for my daughter, too. It was so unfair that she would not have her wonderful brother with her all her life.

We cannot protect others from death, even children. All I could do was to help her express her emotions in whatever way worked – screaming and beating pillows, crying and drawing pictures – but also helping her to remember the good memories and to laugh at the funny stories.

Even yet, my biggest hurt is for my daughter. She is now older than her big brother was when he died, and has grown into a beautiful young woman. It is the milestones – the big birthdays, moving to secondary school – and the ones still to come – leaving school, work, new relationships – that really rip at my heart. All the things I expected them to be together for. The tears can fall easily if I focus on what she has lost, but I can also smile if I choose to remember how much her brother loved her.

Calum's guidance teacher told me (after he had died) of their conversation at his guidance interview with her. She recalled how, when asked about his family, he had said he had a little sister. The teacher asked if they fought, expecting the usual response, but was left smiling when Calum told her, "No, I love her. She's great." Every photo of the two of them together shows him cuddling her. He was so patient, including her in his games, laughing and sharing his friends with her.

Choosing to focus on this helps; my daughter knows she was loved by him. And there are many other stories, written down by Calum's friends, that tell of his love of his sister, his friends and of life. These stories are precious and ensure that he is not forgotten.

It is our connections with other people that matter most in life. Calum had so many friends, he really did create a ripple of fun and laughter around him. He was very kind and caring, generous of spirit and had a strong sense of doing the right thing. His positive impact on others' lives, has even continued beyond his death.

Earlier I told how The Fratellis, Calum's favourite band, had blown me away with their generosity, donating a guitar, painting and drumskin for our fundraising efforts. These great guys became friends as they took action to support us even further. They invited us to take a group of Calum's friends to meet them in their studios. They posed for photographs, signed autographs and spent time talking to the youngsters. They even got some instruments out and we all ended up singing together.

I remember looking around that packed room, at the boys' and girls' smiling faces, and thinking what a good day this was for them and how much Calum would have loved it. Then I noticed Calum's photo on their windowsill. He was smiling amongst us!

The band also went on to dedicate their second album *Here We Stand* to Calum. A very special tribute indeed.

But our connections with The Fratellis also sparked friendship, kindness of spirit, and generosity from their group of fans. We had decided to raffle the guitar, painting and drumskin to raise more funds for the Meningitis Trust, and to hold the draw on Calum's (14th) birthday. The band helped to promote the raffle and many of their fans got in touch with us. They sent us such messages of love and support from all over the world. Some donated prized Fratellis' memorabilia to us, to include in our raffle. One fan in America – a wonderful man called Raf – entered a music competition to win signed Fratellis' goodies. He won and then sent us the prizes. He also wrote to us with such compassion, asking about Calum and sharing in our loss.

Calum's friends helped to organise a Fratellis' music tribute night at his school, to celebrate what would have been his 14th birthday and draw the prized raffle. His friend's bands played on the stage, with those closest to him joining in for a fitting rendition of *Chelsea Dagger* to end the night. The total raised was over £10,000.

The power of doing things for others, of raising money for the Meningitis Trust in tribute to Calum, had really helped us all to gain strength. It had connected people across the globe in love and kindness for a young man they had never met. And helped to knit a cover over the hole in my heart.

These acts of kindness by strangers, family and friends, had a profound effect on us. It was as though a beacon of light had shone through the darkness, and it began to restore my faith in the world.

David R. Hamilton PhD is one of my favourite authors, he writes about the power of the mind and explains the science behind many of the concepts that I believe in. He included my story in his book, "Why Kindness Is Good For You". This gave me a further boost of positive energy, as I knew the kindness I had been shown was spreading even further. I recommend David's books for anyone wanting some "proof" of the power of the mind, body and spirit, in an easy to understand and practical way.

Reflections

There is no right time to stop grieving, nor a right way to grieve. There are stages to go through, emotions to work out, and a new way of living to learn.

Supporting children to come to terms with loss can be especially hard if you are a mother who is grieving. I found that the same advice given to me by my trusted GP also applied to my daughter. Find ways to let go of the emotion, ride the waves, and know that it will get better. Answer questions truthfully and talk about the person who has gone. It helps.

Connecting with others in a shared goal was a truly inspiring time. It wasn't just about the money raised (although that is being put to great use by the charity). It was about the energy, love, compassion and kindness shared. The focus of doing something that could make a difference. This made a difference to our lives, but also to those who heard the stories and shared in the process. Maybe you can find a way to connect and help others, too.

Gather the stories connected to your loved one, ask others to tell their happy memories. You may be surprised to learn some things you never knew.

Words of hope

Even when life seems bleak, the compassion of others can lift you and begin to heal the hole in your heart.

Chapter 8

I expected life to be easier once the first year had passed. I had experienced the loss of loved ones before and thought that once the first set of anniversaries, birthdays and special occasions were past, the next year would be easier. But the grief was still raw at times, and could still surprise me.

I had returned to work – supporting young unemployed people return to work by connecting them with a mentor. I also began to think about my main business, Stress the Positive, and how I could support those who were struggling with difficult times. I knew for certain that I now had a much greater understanding of the low times in life, and that my experiences would allow me to help others so much more. But my confidence was low and I was still on an emotional rollercoaster, so I decided not to work privately with clients until I felt stronger. The last thing anyone needed was me getting upset!

Returning to work was a difficult step; grief seems to rob us of so much. I had always been a confident person, happy to talk to anyone, but those first days back with the mentoring team were really tough. The panic, anxiety and worry were real. Walking into the building to talk to my first group of young people took a lot of courage. I really wondered if I would be able to do it.

I did know that slow breathing would help the feelings of panic, and imagining myself in front of the audience laughing and smiling and feeling good would make it easier. And I was right, that did work.

I did find that I had a much lower tolerance for trouble makers, time wasters, and people who moaned about every little thing or complained about how terrible their life was. It took a lot of effort not to shout at them, "Don't you know how lucky you are? You are alive – you can achieve anything you want to. My son is not here, he doesn't have your chances, so give yourself a shake and make something of your life." I found it better to tell a story instead, and use Calum in a metaphor that would get them thinking.

Experiencing death and loss is a reminder for many of us that life is too short. Many of the little things that used to irritate me no longer mattered. My world was different, but I was back in the "real world" where others still got annoyed about the small stuff. I had to find ways to let go of the frustration and remind myself that others were doing the best they could with what they had available to them.

I began to get out more, to go back to networking and making connections to build up my business. This meant meeting new people and catching up with acquaintances that

I hadn't seen for a while. I have said before, I am a people person, I enjoy meeting new folk, talking to them and sharing stories. But something had changed, Calum's death had really shaken me to my core. Those first few events were really emotional, because I hadn't prepared for the dreaded questions. When meeting someone I knew a little, but hadn't seen for a while, the question was "Where have you been?" or "What have you been doing?"

How did I answer this? Sometimes I told the truth; my son died so I had some time out of work. Sometimes I just said I had been busy with work. It depended on whether I felt able to answer any further questions.

The other dreaded question would come in social discussions. You know the routine – "So what do you do?" often followed by "Do you have any children?"

I struggled to answer this last one. If I said two, then I had to explain that Calum had died; if I said one, it felt like I was being disloyal to my son. It was no longer a simple question. I decided to go with two and explain that Calum had died.

The reaction from others varied. Some asked what happened and wanted to know everything; others recoiled from me with tears in their eyes, as if they could catch my grief or whatever had killed my son. It took a long time before I was comfortable with answering this question. Now I say I have two children – my daughter, Kirsten, is 14, and my son, Calum, died six years ago.

This feels right for me. You have to choose what feels right for you, but I think it helps to have an answer prepared as it lessens the stress, particularly in the early days.

I also had to help my daughter deal with a similar question, "Do you have any brothers or sisters?" I helped her to decide whether she could answer "no", or say "yes, but he died." The choice was left to her with no judgement, just practical help. She decided if the people were going to have an ongoing connection then she would tell them about Calum, but could also say she didn't want to talk about what happened if she didn't feel like it. It was all part of adjusting to our new life as a family of three.

There were other adjustments that needed to be made. What to do with Calum's room and all his things?

It took me a few months to clear Calum's clothes out of his room. I didn't want to part with them, but I knew it was also necessary. I didn't want his room to be a shrine.

I moved his things gradually, putting his clothes in piles – some to be passed on, others kept. His toys could stay there as Kirsten wanted to play with them. She gradually spent more time in his room, sleeping there but still calling it Calum's room. This seemed like a gentler transition – there was no brutal clearing out of all his things. He remained part of us, his collections of cars, swords, cards, action figures, games and books were a reminder of happier times.

I had seen an episode of *Kirsty's Homemade Home* – a TV show where Kirsty Allsop had transformed a run-down house into a home, using traditional crafts. I loved the quilt that Kirsty made and this sparked an idea. A friend told me about someone who had made a memory quilt from clothes, and now I was on a mission.

I wanted to make a memory quilt for Calum. It would be filled with the happy memories of his life, and I would ask his friends and family to make squares and be a part of it. It would be a celebration of all that he had been, and filled with love for all that he had meant to so many. The only problem I had – I didn't know how to make a quilt.

I found a class in Glasgow, learned the techniques required, and discovered a hobby that I love. Making a quilt is great therapy; creating a plan, choosing colours and fabrics, cutting, stitching and seeing it grow, requires your attention. It's almost like meditation – you can switch off from everything else around. Then there is the satisfaction of the end result.

Once I had made my first quilt, I embarked on persuading my friends and family that they could make a square to tell of their memories of Calum. I had a huge list of all the things he had enjoyed, the holidays we shared, the qualities that made him who he was. It was a challenge to fit all of this into a quilt. Sourcing material, learning new ways to sew, how to print onto fabric, and decide on how to pull it all together, proved to be a group effort.

This was a therapeutic project but also a tough one at times. The help from family and friends – especially Jane – in helping to make it happen, meant a lot. I just love it, and think the end result is wonderful.

The back of the quilt is Calum's duvet cover, so not only does it tell his life story but it has a real connection to him. I love it so much, I can wrap it around me when I want comfort, and look at it when I want to remember the stories.

I hope it will be passed on to Kirsten, and maybe her family in years to come.

"Calum's Quilt" – the story of his life

Calum is also remembered in his school, Bishopbriggs Academy. Our wonderful friends, Alan and Lorna Berry, donated a trophy in Calum's memory and it is awarded every year to a pupil who is a good citizen. It is so pleasing that he is remembered in this way and that a pupil is given recognition for being a kind person who helps others. We have attended the prizegiving ceremony every year to see the pupils who have been awarded the trophy. It is a bittersweet experience, but I am glad that Calum is not forgotten.

I have mentioned before that Calum had a wonderful group of friends, and they also ensured that he was not forgotten as they entered their last year of school. Each sixth year group chooses a charity to raise money for throughout their final school year. There was no question: this would be the Meningitis Trust, and all the money would be raised in Calum's memory.

S6 pupils Bishopbriggs Academy, and spell out Calum's name.

This great group of kids arranged lots of fun activities and events to raise money. They had a sleepover in the school, playing games, racing go karts, and playing music all night. The teachers gave up their night, too, and supported the whole event which was so very touching for us.

On what would have been Calum's 17th birthday, his friends decided to have a memorial service at the school. We were invited to attend and sat in awe as this wonderful group of young men and women talked of their happy memories of Calum and of how much he was missed. They then showed us a video that they had made themselves, in which they had interviewed more of his friends and teachers. They had even gone to his primary school and interviewed his old teachers, asking for their memories and stories. The film was a real tribute to my son, but also a tribute to the love and power of friendship. There was not a dry eye in the hall as we watched this wonderful film with the teachers and his friends. The Head Teacher struggled to speak as he praised this wonderful group of young people for what they had done.

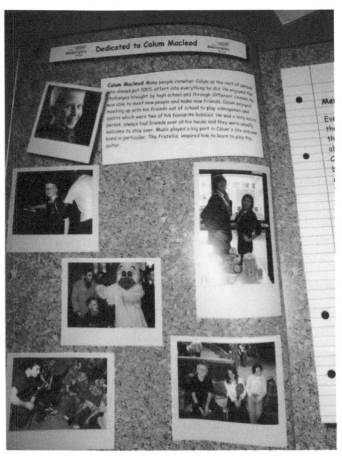

Calum was not left out of their Year Book, either. The committee of young people producing the book made sure that he had a full page dedicated to him.

Too often the young people of our society are described as neds, not interested in anything, cynical and harsh. It is my privilege to say that Calum's friends are some of the most wonderful young people, and their compassion and kindness has really made such a difference to our lives.

Keeping Calum's memory alive is very important to me. Talking about him and sharing the stories of his life with us, celebrates his existence. The fact that an amazing group of young people and teachers also chose to keep his memory alive, fills me with pride and lights up my soul.

I know that some people find it difficult to talk about loss and come to terms with it. Calum's friends were only 12 and 13 when they were faced with the harsh reality of death. I think that, because they were given opportunities to grieve but also to do something positive, it helped them to cope.

Calum's Deputy Head Teacher Moira Carberry spoke at his funeral. She said, "They say you can tell a man by the company he keeps, and Calum's choice of friends showed what type of boy he was… courteous, polite and unassuming, showing kindness and genuine concern for others. A decent boy through and through."

His friends continue to show these same qualities today. I thank them for the joy and laughter they shared with Calum and for their continued love and kindness.

Reflections

There are many things to adapt to when you experience loss. Deep grief can shake you to your core and this can have a profound impact on your life. Things that you did with ease, now may seem difficult. The confidence you had may feel like it has deserted you. Little things that used to bother you are no longer worth thinking about. Your life has changed but the lives of others around you may not. Even the people closest to you may return back to their "normal" state after a time.

I don't think this is a lack of empathy or about not caring, it is about preserving their world. You know how difficult your world feels now and those around you will have felt the aftershock of it but long for the comfort of normal. They have the luxury of being able to do so. You have to create a new normal; this takes time and understanding.

Being kind to yourself and being prepared to face difficult stages, are all part of returning to life. Finding the courage to talk about your loss as part of your life, helps you to heal. Acknowledging your loved one will always be part of your life helps you to stay connected.

You may not want to make a quilt, but you can find other ways to connect with the positive times with your loved one, their loves and laughter. Scrap books, memory boxes, written stories, photo journals are all ways to remember them in life. Whatever caused their death is not your loved one, and when you can look back and focus on their life rather than their death, it keeps that memory alive and can help you to live now.

Words of hope

Pushing through the difficult times increases your confidence and makes it easier next time round.

The life of your loved one is more important than their death. Find ways to connect and remember the happier times. It fuels your soul, too.

Chapter 9

Two years since Calum's death and my energy levels were not back to normal. I found regular household cleaning even more of a chore than ever. Grief drains you physically and emotionally. But the normality of life trundles on, with money worries, bills to pay, and health and family issues to deal with. I wanted to scream at the injustice of it all: my son was dead, I didn't want to deal with anything else. I didn't want to visit the hospital, or care for another sick person.

But life carried on, the normality of it all kept going around us, and I know that others didn't understand how I felt. You may have experienced times in life where it is just one thing after another that goes wrong, or that you have to deal with. Each one of us has a breaking point – a time when life seems to be too much. It can be a series of small things, or one or two big events. I know that my resistance was low and the small everyday things that I once would have coped with now seemed like huge mountains.

Writing helped. I continued to write to Calum, pouring out my feelings and telling him my worries. I wrote down the thoughts that I didn't want to admit to others. I'd cry and get upset, then it felt better. I'd then write about happier times and recall good memories, and this lifted my mood. I returned to some of my earlier practices of using aromatherapy oils and crystals to shift my mood.

I knew that I had to lift my emotions; I was aware that when I felt happier, I coped better with the other "stuff" of life. At those times, I could handle the emotional ups and downs of others and have a different perspective on it all.

The fundraising efforts helped give me a boost, but now I had to concentrate on connecting with my life again. It was time to plan for the future, get active, and think about how I could use what I had learned; to really create something useful from my experiences.

Plan for the future! That was proving a difficult one. As someone who used to drive everyone to distraction with plans and lists, I had abandoned plans. What was the point in planning? I hadn't scheduled my son's death into my five year plan. But by closing down that essence of myself, I had closed down the part that could hope and look forward to things, the part that went beyond the plans and actually made things happen. So I began to explore what I wanted to do.

Life is for living and enjoying. It is important to do the things that add to that, and that meant my work too. Sinclair has taken this approach to heart. His IT career had been stressful and he had left this to start his own website business a few months before Calum died.

Sinclair's love of books and writing had always been in the background, but Calum's death had made him re-evaluate what he really wanted to do. He committed to writing and finishing a novel; he now knew that life is too short, so he did not want to put off his dreams any longer.

I am so proud of my husband for taking this approach. He did finish his first book, "The Reluctant Detective", and self published it. (He has gone on to write and publish five more books, selling over 75,000 copies.) We talked a lot about how he wished he had done this years ago and that Calum had read his books. But if Calum had not died, maybe Sinclair would never have written them.

This is a challenge for us all at times – how to create something positive after such a dark and difficult time. How to find the energy and motivation to push ourselves out of the low energy that we feel.

This is where I began to focus my thoughts. I had used many different techniques to lift my thoughts and mood. I knew how to let go of the negative emotions, instead of holding on to them. I knew from real experience what made a difference to my life. Happiness was the elusive state that many people wanted, but didn't know how to find. This was something I could focus on. I could help people to bring more happiness into their lives. To brighten up the darkness and add more light and colour to their world.

Even the thoughts of adding more happiness to the world inspired me. I felt energised and hopeful; this was something that I could do. It was connected to the ideas I had had for Stress the Positive when I started it a couple of years earlier, but now it was beginning to burn like a passion. But the question was how? How would I do it? What would work best? What did others do?

Now with the beginning of an idea, I began to notice the thoughts that would pop into my head. I came across articles and programmes that others had produced. I would turn on the TV and some programme would be discussing alternative ways to beat depression. I bumped into people who shared their stories. I found books to read and online resources to connect with. It was as if the universe was driving things towards me.

If you have come across the Law of Attraction, you may have read about this sort of experience before. As my focus was on creating happiness, I was drawing opportunities, people and resources to me that could help. I felt my energy lift as a result. But I also felt overwhelmed at times and had doubts, too.

I questioned what people would think of me – was it right to step into this role and use what I had experienced? I also looked at what other people were doing – those with successful businesses – and questioned whether I could really do this.

It's normal to have doubts and fears. But I thought of Calum and what he would say to me. "Go for it, Mum, you can do this and make a real difference," I heard in my thoughts. And so the Happiness Club began to move from just an idea into reality.

Reflections

Learning to live and enjoy life again takes time. There are many things that contribute to this. Finding some passion in life makes it worthwhile. As I look back over the last few years of my life, I am aware of the difference which connecting with my passion for helping others has made to me. It has given me a lot of joy and brought me into contact with a huge number of people.

This has also been true for Sinclair. Writing his books and helping other writers to publish has helped him to cope with the loss of our son.

This is not a linear journey; there are still times when we have low spells. But finding our passion, some way to use our pain and loss to transport us to achieve something that we may never have done, is a true testament to our love for Calum, Kirsten, and ourselves. It is about saying that life does not end, the hurt can be made easier, and the hole in our hearts can be knitted over to allow us to live well and be happy.

It does take effort; it takes commitment to life. To honour the dead by living well. I know many have struggled with this. I have heard many stories of people who have shut themselves away after losing a loved one – mothers who never got over the death of their child; husbands who shut themselves away after losing their wife; children who continue to grieve for lost siblings, or parents. Death affects us all. But the death of our loved ones does not need to be the death of our lives, too.

Finding some passion for life, in whatever form, begins to bring more life and happiness to you.

Words of Hope

Consider what you enjoy in life. What you have put off or would love to do. Begin to think about what it would be like to do this, or to have this. See this as an opportunity to heal your pain and honour your loved one.

If you were to die, would you want your loved ones to celebrate your life by living the life that would make them happy?

It all begins with a thought ...

Part Three

Life Gets Better

Chapter 10

The Happiness Club opened its doors in April 2011. As I mentioned earlier, I had found lots of information, and inspiration had come into my sphere of awareness – the organisation, Action for Happiness, was to be my catalyst.

I became aware of the launch of the UK charity through the Happiness Challenge that they were running on BBC TV. The charity was encouraging people to take the pledge to increase happiness and take action. And this is what I decided to do. Action for Happiness was launching their charity in April 2011 and I decided that I would start a class at the same time.

It's amazing once a decision is made how things can change. When you are stuck in no-man's land of indecision, so much energy is used up debating and weighing up the pros and cons, thinking through all that could be good or what can go wrong. If your energy is low, it's no wonder that you don't get around to taking action. What I found was that once I had made the decision to have my first happiness club night, my energy changed. My passion was engaged; I was feeling excited about something and now I had focus.

So how did I start something new? I talked to some friends that I thought would like to spend an evening exploring what made us happier. I rounded up ten people to try out my idea, found a venue, and arranged the evening. It was a bit nerve wracking and the doubts were there, but the excitement and passion were greater. The first night was a great success – my friends loved it, and so did I. I was truly happy; buoyant from the experience, the effort and the feedback. I knew that the Happiness Club would be a success for those coming along, but also for me.

However, I don't want you to think that everything just fell into place and life was sorted. No, it wasn't like that. Creating the Happiness Club meant a commitment to producing materials, marketing it, and engaging with people. I had lots of ideas for topics and material to use – the Club was to be a mix of practical ways to boost happiness. It would be a place to open up to new ideas and learning, about alternative therapies, how your mind works, how emotions are connected to thoughts, and how to change them. I would share NLP, hypnotherapy, Emotional Freedom Technique, colour therapy and positive psychology.

But it was important to me that all the sessions were real and authentic, recognising that life can be hard, bad things do happen, and that I wasn't advocating people should just put on a smile and pretend everything was okay.

I knew that a lot of the American style of personal development would not quite fit with our Scottish culture.

Scots can be seen as dour and miserable, but we have a fabulous sense of humour and a "just get on with it" attitude. I set about creating a way to bring together my knowledge and experiences with the great messages from personal development, spiritual and positive psychology writers, presenting it to the Glasgow people in a fun and upbeat way. But at times I found myself struggling with being "Mrs Happy" and Kim – the mum who had lost her son. Thoughts that I should be perfectly happy all the time to run a happiness club conflicted with the reality of life as a bereaved mum.

Guilt – it's a small word but can have huge consequences. I didn't want to talk constantly about my loss; this was the Happiness Club, it wasn't a grief counselling or depression support group. Yet it was focused on real life, so I shared bits of my journey on occasions. On the other hand, I didn't want people to think that I was over Calum's death and was now happy all the time. It was a bit of a balancing act.

I wanted to live happily, but my concern for how others would see this niggled away at me. Maybe you have felt this too – fearful of being judged for getting on with life. It wasn't rational, it was emotional. Even with my knowledge of how my thoughts, beliefs and view of the world worked together to create the emotion, I still felt it.

If I hadn't been aware of what was going on in my head, it would probably have stopped me from continuing with the Happiness Club. Have you stopped yourself from doing something because you were worried about what others would think? Or you just felt guilty and didn't know why? The reality is, I didn't know what others thought – I was mind-reading and imagining. But when I looked at this from another perspective, I realised that I was helping people to see that life does go on. The very ideas that I had been teaching (honouring our loved ones by living our lives well) would be shown in practical ways by developing the Happiness Club further.

I settled into the belief that I didn't have to be happy all the time to be able to teach others how to become happier. No-one is happy 24/7, but we can all aim to be happy more of the time. This resolved the conflict and guilt that I had been feeling. It freed me up to acknowledge the difficult days and share more about what worked for me. I didn't need a mask, and I think that this real life approach to happiness is what has made the Happiness Club so successful.

How can you apply any of this to your life? If you have found a passion for something and want to nurture that feeling, share it with others. A word of caution though – choose carefully who you share with. Share your ideas with the people who you know will be encouraging and supportive, not the ones who will only see all the flaws or difficulties of your ideas and suggest you best leave it alone. Gather one or two people together and explore how you could add more of your passions to your life, explain how it makes you feel alive again, and ask them to help you to do it.

Helping others makes you feel good. This does not mean that *you* have to help others (although you can); this is a reminder that asking others to help you actually gives people an opportunity to do something that makes *them* feel good. I know I'm not alone in being the first to offer to help others yet the last to ask for help for myself. Shifting my perspective on this really works for me.

Acknowledge that there may still be times when you feel low or guilty for enjoying life again. Feelings are not always logical. If it occurs, ask yourself: what would my son/daughter/husband/wife/partner say if they were here now? Remind yourself that you are honouring their memory by finding enjoyment, and could be inspiring others to live their lives well, too.

Spend time with positive people. One reason the Happiness Club boosts my happiness is that we are all focused on a positive outcome and enjoy laughing together. Boost your positive energy by laughing and sharing your time with upbeat people.

Congratulate yourself on moving forward, on achieving something, and then you can begin to pursue more ways to add happiness to your life.

Reflections

Having the thought about sharing my experiences and knowledge was the beginning. It took fuel and energy to get it going and, when I made the decision to create the Happiness Club, my life and emotional wellbeing improved.

You must remember that healing from grief is not a linear process, and even several years down the line I still experienced some difficult emotions as I pursued a happier life through my passion for helping others.

I continued to write and talk with Calum; it helped to make sense of my feelings and to ask him what he thought. I would "hear" answers in my head that encouraged me to continue. Whatever your beliefs are about life beyond death, you can imagine what your loved one would say to you if you were asking for their help. The people that truly love you want the best for you. It is only your imagination about what others may be thinking that can stop you. More often than not, other people give our lives very little thought and attention. So, if your new-found passion in life is a complete change of career, a new location, travelling, or learning new skills, and it makes you feel alive and happy – embrace it.

Words of hope

Life can be happy and fulfilling again. Life is for living, no-one is guaranteed tomorrow, so use your experience of grief and loss to make a difference and choose to be happy.

Chapter 11

Having found enjoyment, a sense of purpose and laughter in my life again, the down days are less. I still miss Calum and the hole in my heart still exists, but I believe I have knitted a cover for it by being happy. Making the choice to be happy, taking small steps, being patient and kind to myself, asking for help, letting go of the emotion, finding my passion and deciding to follow it, are the strands that have knitted together.

Life continues in all its richness, and that means the normal ups, downs and challenges of family life are to celebrated, survived, and faced, in due course. Grief and loss has changed my perspective on what is important and what isn't worth worrying or getting annoyed about, but that doesn't mean that I bounce along all the time.

What I have established is that happiness gives you bounce-ability. Finding ways to add more happiness to my life hasn't stopped bad things from happening, but it helps me to cope and bounce back quicker.

I have developed my own Bag of Happiness as a fun way to store and remind me of what makes me happy. The idea behind this came from a children's book which I had read to both Calum and Kirsten. *My Huge Bag of Worries*, by Virginia Ironside, is the story of a little girl who carries all her worries with her in an ever-increasing bag. She eventually manages to share her worries, and empties the bag. It is a good story and a great way to explore letting go of worries, but I was left wondering: what do you do with the empty bag? I decided to fill it with happiness instead!

I developed this idea into a workshop for both children and adults, and have used this with hundreds of people. I love the fun aspect of making/decorating the bag, but it is the content that makes it special. Each bag of happiness is unique because it is yours – your memories, hopes, dreams, ideas, etc. It's not about clever techniques or complicated strategies. It is a way to help you connect with your own happiness, and a reminder of what can work to help you bounce back when you feel low or are going through a tough time. It is resilience in a bag.

I have included the guide to make your own Bag of Happiness at the end of this book, so I'd urge you to take some time and have fun with this. You could create it with your family and friends, or on your own. All you need is a bag – a paper one, a cotton one, or a hand bag; any will do.

Creating the space to think about happy times frees you from feeling bad. It may seem like an obvious point, but how often have you thought about what makes you happy? It's not a question that many people ask, and it's all the more important when you feel unhappy.

If you are still in the early days of grief or loss, or feeling utterly miserable, then happiness may seem very far away. The perception from many people I have worked with is that it will take them a long time to feel better, they think they will have to work hard to be happy, some believe they may never feel happy again. It is so rewarding to see someone smile and laugh within a few minutes of making their own Bag of Happiness. This doesn't mean that all their problems are solved, or that they will be eternally happy from now on, but it has created a space to allow some happiness into their lives again.

This simple approach acknowledges that it's good to feel happy, and gives you a route to explore some of this in a structured way. You can start now, if you have a few minutes or a few hours; it's up to you.

Choosing to focus on your own happiness is a way to help you help others, too. If you've ever travelled on an aeroplane, you'll have heard the flight attendants advise that in the event of loss of cabin pressure, oxygen masks will drop from above your head – FIX YOUR OWN MASK FIRST BEFORE HELPING OTHERS. Choosing to increase your happiness is like fixing your own oxygen supply. It will give you the energy to help cope with life.

When you feel more positive you can spread this to others, your emotions do transfer; if you smile, people smile back – it's an automatic response. If you are also supporting other family members or friends through loss, you need energy. Laughter, smiles and positive feelings give you energy; they lift you physically as well as emotionally.

Increasing your happiness helps you to feel better physically, too. Feeling happy produces chemical changes in your body – the extra dopamine and serotonin (feel-good chemicals) have a positive impact on your health. There are lots of studies which highlight the link between positive emotion and healthy hearts. Studies have also shown that heart cells can repair themselves. If you have experienced loss and heartache, then maybe the hole that you feel really is being healed in this way.

Happiness reduces the stress that can surround us all at times. High levels of stress can be reduced quickly with a thought, a few smiles, and some positive emotions. But finding the thought, that smile of happiness, can be difficult when all you can think about is how bad your situation is. This is why I love my Bag of Happiness. I know where I can look for a smile, a positive memory, or find some laughter. It is a starting point, a reminder, and an ongoing approach – all rolled up in one.

I like simple things. The easier things are to do, the more likely I am to do them. All the concepts within the Bag of Happiness are simple; they can be found in many other teachings, they are practical and they will work for you. Once you have created your own Bag of Happiness, you have your own happiness first aid kit at your fingertips. It's your place to go to fix your own oxygen supply. When you feel low, you can withdraw something from your bag – memories, music, laughter, dreams, kindness, gratitude; there is a whole range to choose from. I know from experience that different things work on different days. Choosing and using the happiness you put in will boost your mood now.

When you feel happier, your situation looks a little different, your perception will change and allow you to consider different ways to think, feel and act. When you follow this route regularly, your internal roadmap starts to change. You can find your way to a happier life more easily. And the more you practise, the easier it gets.

Reflections

Creating my Bag of Happiness really helped me to focus on the things that could help me to shift my perspective and feel happier. Feeling happier won't change the situation, but it does make life more pleasant. And your Bag of Happiness is something to add to – it's a metaphor for your life, a way of noticing and storing the positive aspects that make a difference. You add more happiness as time goes on, and use it to give you a boost during difficult times. The trick is to use the contents to make a difference.

I find that music and memories are the fast boosters for me. Playing my happy tunes and remembering a happy time will lift my spirits quickly. Other aspects give longer lasting results – you may find new things or different experiences work for you. Play around with it and learn from it, as this is the best investment you can make. It doesn't cost you any money, it's simple and easy to use, and makes your life happier.

Words of hope

You can feel happier in an instant with your own Bag of Happiness. Smiles and laughter can be yours again.

Chapter 12

At the end of 2011, the Happiness Club was growing and I had this feeling that I should take the message further. There was a World Happy Day scheduled for February 2012, and I started to think that Scotland should have its own Happiness Day.

I wanted to share the message that each of us can make a difference; we can increase our own happiness and help those around us, too. The media often focuses so much on the doom and gloom of life, the economy and conflict. Faced with all this negativity, it is no wonder that people feel low and helpless.

I had this dream of people around the country getting involved – sharing their day with others, being active and adding in acts of kindness. So Scotland's Happiness Day was born.

Together with some enthusiastic friends and Happiness Club members, we began to form ideas for a Happiness Conference. The date was chosen as 10th November 2012

– as this date would read 10.11.12. It was easy to remember, a dateline never to be repeated in our lifetime, and the darkness of winter nights would be drawing in.

Getting this project off the ground required the four Es - effort, energy, enthusiasm and engagement. I love when a new project starts, I love the ideas, enthusiasm and energy it generates, but the effort to engage others beyond our group was a real challenge.

As the day drew closer, I was getting more exhausted by the amount of work needed and the effort to sell tickets, market the day, and get the Scottish media involved. I was also heading through the 5th anniversary of Calum's death and doing a fundraising challenge, walking 5k every day for 50 days. It's no wonder that I felt as if I was on my knees as the Happiness Day drew closer.

I had certainly given myself a huge challenge, and was feeling the emotional strain of it. It was like our first fundraising event after Calum's death; the highs and lows were coming in waves. I had to do the one thing that I have admitted before is not easy for me – ask for help! And when I did, my wonderful friends came to the rescue again, from helping with ticket sales and practical help organising parts of the day, to contacting the media to get some interest going. The shift in energy was amazing and the day turned out to be a great success.

It reminded me once again that allowing others to help made such a difference to me and to them. (A lesson I am still working on!)

In March 2012, for the first UN International Day of Happiness, I was awarded a Happy Hero medal by Action for Happiness, in recognition of the work that I had done to spread happiness. This was a great honour, and I had a fabulous day in London at the House of Lords. It is wonderful to be thanked for making a difference in the world.

My Happy Hero medal was to be passed on to someone who I considered a Happy Hero, and I chose my good friend, Margaret McCathie. She is a wonderfully warm and caring person, who has spread joy and laughter throughout the world in spite of her own health problems. Although I will admit to feeling a little upset at not being able to keep the medal, Margaret was a deserving recipient. The medal has since been passed on another four times to other happy heroes.

Kim passes on the Happy Hero medal to Margaret McCathie

Being recognised and thanked for being happy made me feel great, and also sparked another idea! I could add an awards ceremony to Scotland's Happiness Day celebrations.

And so, as I write this, the Smile Awards have just been launched across Scotland with the help of local newspaper group, Johnston Press. With a network of local newspapers and websites, they have helped to spread the word to communities around Scotland. Nominations are already flooding in, as people thank their friends, neighbours, family and community, for helping them to smile.

Reading the nominations has been really touching; people around the country being thanked for being kind, helpful, full of good cheer and laughter, encouraging and supportive. The awards seem to have captured people's hearts and minds already. I know that they will make a difference and add more happiness – the person being thanked will be happy, but the person giving thanks gets a boost, too.

I have a difficult task ahead to whittle down the nominations to 11 regional winners, who will be guests of honour at the Happiness Day conference on 2 November 2013. They will each be presented with a Smile Award medal to keep.

Scotland's Happiness Day is growing this year; the conference in Glasgow is bigger and, with the media's help, I am sure that people around the country will get involved. It is very exciting and rewarding to think of how many people this could encourage to be happier. (See www. scotlandshappinessday.com for more information.)

As you can see – from one positive thought, the gem of an idea is then fanned with the flames of hope, encouragement, friends, laughter and happiness, to make a difference which can change your life and that of those around you.

Reflections

Who could you thank today? Who has helped you to smile and laugh? Is there someone who brightens your day with their cheery nature, laughter and goodwill? If you are in Scotland, then maybe you can nominate them for a Smile Award; if not, then write them a letter. Thank them for what they do, for how they brighten your day, and say how it makes you feel. You could take it to them and read it, or post it as a surprise.

Words of Hope

The tiniest of ideas can grow into action that can help you and others. What would you like to see change? What would you like to be remembered for?

Final thoughts

It's almost six years now since Calum died. I have learned so much about what helps me to feel happier, and have encouraged others to do the same.

Maybe I could have achieved everything I have without losing Calum, but I would not have been able to understand the depths of despair or the highs and lows of grief in the same way. I may not have appreciated the power of kindness in a smile, and a connection with people, in the same way.

This journey has made me ask questions about life and death, and has opened my mind and heart to possibilities that I may never have considered. If I had a choice, undoubtedly I would have Calum back; but that is not the choice I have. The choice I have is to live well, be happy and make something good come from my experiences, or to hold onto the despair and anger at life for not being what I wanted.

If you have lost a loved one, been affected by illness, relationship difficulties, or experienced tragedy or an unwelcome change in your life, then this is your choice, too.

I hope that I have given you some courage to be happy, and some ways to do it. You don't have to like what has happened to accept it and create a happier life. It is your choice.

Everyone's journey through life will be full of good times and bad. A lady once said to me that she didn't want to get too happy because something bad always happened. I know that bad things happen, but the good times make life enjoyable. I believe that it's better to be happy, to make good memories, to enjoy life to the full, to laugh daily, to share your smiles, laughter and happiness, and to help others.

Happiness gives you bounce-ability; it really can help you to handle those low times. Once you understand what can boost your happiness, then you can be in control of bouncing back faster.

And our emotions transfer to others; so spreading happiness is a real joy.

I want to leave you with one of my favourite poems.

Calum and Kim - smiles all round

THE SMILE STARTER

Smiling is infectious,
You catch it like the flu.
When someone smiled at me today,
I started smiling, too.
I passed around the corner,
And someone saw me grin.
When he smiled, I realised,
I'd passed it on to him.
I thought about that smile,
Then I realised its worth.
A single smile just like mine,
Could travel round the earth.
So if you feel a smile begin,
Don't leave it undetected.
Let's start an epidemic quick,
And get the world infected.
(author unknown)

I truly wish you a good life, good health and happiness.

Kim x

Part Four

Your Turn

10 Quick and Easy Happiness Boosters

Use these easy tips to brighten your mood with little effort.

1. Look up – sit upright in a chair, with your shoulders back, and look up towards the ceiling. Breathe deeply for a few minutes.

2. Smell a fragrance you love. Essential oils or perfumes, favourite foods or flowers. Even imagining you can smell it can help.

3. Surround yourself with colour. Colours such as red, orange and yellow have been associated with boosting mood and energy.

4. Read some positive quotes, jokes or funny stories.

5. Smile even if you don't feel like it.

6. Imagine yourself sitting in your favourite place with the sun shining. Make it real in your mind, hear the sounds, feel the physical sensations, and enjoy the view.

7. Listen to some upbeat music – especially good if it makes you dance and sing.

8. Go for a short walk. Fresh air and exercise can make such a difference.

9. Phone a cheerful friend for a quick chat or, even better, have a cup of tea with them.

10. Give someone a cuddle. A pet, cuddly toy or favourite blanket can work, too.

*Your own supply of happiness
whenever you want it*

Creating your bag of happiness

There is no magical pill that can create happiness. You can choose to have a happy life; you just need to know how to do it. I have filled this Bag of Happiness with lots of the tips, techniques and know-how that I have used personally and have also shared with hundreds of others.

Many people have made their own Bags of Happiness at one of my workshops. I have had great fun sharing this simple idea with people, and I hope that you will enjoy it as much as I do.

Think of this bag as your personal supply of real life happiness. It will be filled with your own memories, hopes and ideas. It's your first step to increasing happiness in your life.

Happiness is...

What makes the world a better place. It makes life worth living. It is the icing on the cake.

Happiness is...

Good for your health – happy people have 32% less stress hormones, and are 22% less likely to get heart disease.

Happiness is...

Contagious! Our emotions transfer to others, so focusing on your happiness is good for others, too.

Happiness is...

Something you can achieve. What you think, focus on, and do, affects you. You can be happier but sometimes you need a little helping hand – or a bag!

We all want to be happy, but sometimes life gets in the way.

Feeling unhappy?

If you are stressed, worried, or feel low, happiness may seem out of reach. It is common to focus on your problems and feel like it is too hard to make life better.

You may have a lot of resources to help, but your attention isn't on them. Creating and filling your very own Bag of Happiness will make sure that you have your personal supply of happiness whenever you need it.

The Science of Happiness

In recent years, research has developed in positive psychology and happiness.

Positive psychology looks at how happy people are and measures what they think, focus on, and do. It is accepted that you can learn how to be happier, not just less miserable.

Our potential for happiness is influenced by various factors.

Our genetics and upbringing account for 50%; interestingly, our income and environment account for only 10%; and our daily activities and relationships 40%.

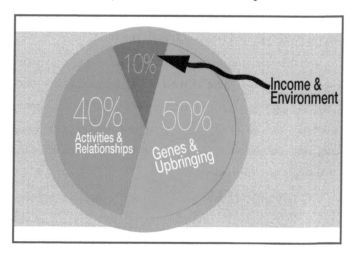

This means that even if you have miserable parents and not a lot of money, you can still be happy!

Martin Seligman, Professor of Positive Psychology at Pennsylvania University, has also identified that how we view and feel about our past, present and future affects our happiness.

You cannot change what has happened in the past, you may not be able to control or change your present circumstances, but you can change how you think, feel and react now. You can do something different and we are going to explore how.

Over the years, you will have developed habits and ways of thinking, but it is possible to change and develop new ones that make you happier. Your brain can adapt to your new ways of thinking, making it easier for you.

The world of Neuroscience has also evolved and we now know that our brain continues to grow and develop new neural pathways and connections all the time.

It's like driving your car on the same route to work every day. One day there's a road block and you get diverted. Suddenly you see a whole new road and find the journey more pleasant. After a few days, this route becomes the usual one, and you choose to keep taking this road even after the roadworks are finished.

Your brain can adapt and create new routes to happiness.

Neuro Linguistic Programming

I love NLP; the techniques offer a great way to take control of your thoughts, emotions and reactions. I see people achieving great results by using these techniques every day. You are going to use a few NLP techniques while making your Bag of Happiness.

Did you know that your mind and body are connected?

When you experience something, your mind absorbs all the information, then filters, rejects or deletes aspects based on your previous experiences, your beliefs and values.

You have some feeling about the situation and you will react in some way.

But your mind does not know the difference between something that is physically happening and some idea or mind video that you are playing in your head. So your body will react as if the situation is actually happening.

You have probably experienced a time when you really scared yourself silly just thinking and worrying about something. You maybe didn't know that you could also use this same process to feel happy instead.

Using NLP techniques, you can use your imagination and create your own ideas that will make you feel good. You can change how you feel about a past event and react differently now or in future. You can use good experiences from the past to help you feel good now. And you can create what you want to happen in your mind, to improve optimism in the future.

Check out my website (www.stressthepositive.co.uk) for more info.

Okay so far? That's the theory and science bit, now for some practical ways to feel better.

Measuring your Happiness

For many years psychologists measured how depressed or stressed you were, then explored how to make you less depressed.

Thankfully, the positive psychology specialists decided it was important to take a more positive perspective and developed assessments to measure how happy you are. This can be a useful starting point on your journey of happiness. The General Happiness Scale was developed by Professor Martin Seligman and has been used with thousands of people. (visit www.authentichappiness.com)

There are many other assessment methods you can find on his site.

This assessment is a simple way to rate your general happiness with life just now.

For each of the following statements or questions, please circle the point on the scale that you feel is most appropriate in describing you at this time.

In general, I consider myself:

Not a very happy person   Not a very happy person

1   2   3   4   5   6   7

Compared to most of my peers, I consider myself:

Less happy   More happy

1   2   3   4   5   6   7

Some people are generally very happy. They enjoy life, regardless of what is going on, getting most out of everything. To what extent does this describe you?

Not at all   A great deal

1   2   3   4   5   6   7

Some people are generally not very happy. Although they are not depressed, they never seem as happy as they might be. To what extent does this describe you?

A Great Deal   Not at all

1   2   3   4   5   6   7

To score the test, add your results together then divide by 4.

My General Happiness Score is   *on*   *(date)*

Two thirds of people score between 3.8 and 5.8.

In other words, if your score is greater than 5.8, you are more happy than two-thirds of the people who take this test.

If your score is less than 3.8, then you are less happy than two-thirds of the people taking the test.

You can redo this test periodically, and see how your levels of happiness can grow with action.

NOW let's focus on creating more happiness.

What makes you happy?

What makes you feel happy, content or full of joy, is different from person to person. We all like different things, different activities; we get on with some people better than others.

I love going out for picnics with my family, talking and laughing with my friends, walking by the sea, reading, learning new things. What about you?

Spend a few minutes thinking about what you enjoy doing and who you have in your life now that adds to your happiness?

Decorate your Bag of Happiness.

This is the fun part; it's time to decorate your bag. Let out your creative side, be colourful, and make it look happy!

Add your name, draw a picture, add some stickers to it, and maybe even a bit of sparkle. Whatever you like – it's your bag.

Filling your bag with happiness

Now you are going to fill your bag with happiness to hold the thoughts, memories, ideas and suggestions that will help you feel confident, happy and able to deal with all the challenges that life can throw at you.

Get comfortable, switch off the phone, and create some space. Give yourself permission to take the first step to creating a happier life. Have fun, use your imagination and enjoy the experience.

There is space for you to write your ideas and memories in this section of the book. You can use more paper if you want to add more to your bag.

You can draw pictures, use photographs, or add mementoes, to help you connect with your past memories/achievements. It is your bag, so you choose.

I suggest that you complete these pages and fill your bag in one session. It will take around half an hour, or maybe longer if you are really enjoying it.

Right – let's get cracking. It's time to fill up your bag.

Happy Memories

Have you ever talked about happy past events with your family and friends, and ended up laughing? I do it a lot.

Have you noticed how good you feel? You can create this feeling for yourself. When you remember good times, you may have a picture in your head like you are dreaming, you may hear the sounds/voices. Relive this happy time and your body will react as if it is happening again – giving you an instant boost of happiness.

Add 3 happy memories to your bag.

1.

2.

3.

What have you done to make you feel proud?

It is good to acknowledge what you have achieved. It boosts your self-confidence.

When you feel low, it's easy to lose sight of things you have done well. If you are stressed, the list of things you still have to do can be overwhelming.

Taking time to remember your achievements returns your focus to the positive. Whether you made a great cake, ran a marathon, stopped smoking, or passed exams, recognise it as an achievement and be proud.

Add 3 achievements to your bag.

1.

2.

3.

Strengths, good points and more

You have strengths and things you are good at, but you can forget these in times of stress. You may have aspects of your character that you don't like – but you are not a slave to these. You can change your behaviour.

What characteristics and strengths do you have that you admire and like? Are you friendly, helpful, open-minded, brave? Don't be modest; think about what you can do and build on these.

Add 3 things you like to your bag.

1.

2.

3.

Things to look forward to.

Having something to look forward to can make a difference to how happy you feel. Most of us look forward to the weekend, or a holiday. The sense of anticipation of having fun and enjoying ourselves can keep us going through a tough day at work or a cold winter.

It doesn't have to be big things, either – meeting a friend, getting the time to read a good book, or a having a great cup of tea are all things that I look forward to.

Add 3 things you are looking forward to into your bag.

1.

2.

3.

An attitude of gratitude

Being grateful for what you have shifts your focus away from the things you don't have.

Studies have shown that developing a practice of gratitude has helped people to beat depression and feel happier.

Gratitude shifts your perspective and attitude to life. So what – or who - do you have to be grateful for in your life now? Take a couple of minutes and see how many things you can come up with to add to your bag. Aim to add more every day.

I am grateful for...

Let out your inner child – it's fun to play

When you were a child, you may have spent your days playing – creating wonderfully imaginative worlds in cardboard boxes, making mud pie dinners, and having tea parties with teddies. Can you create that same fun as an adult?

Taking time to play and have fun is good for all of us. Life doesn't have to be serious all the time. If you have a tub of Play-Doh, make a model of something that makes you happy, or blow bubbles!

Get creative: add 3 ways you can add more fun to your life.

1.

2.

3.

Music can boost your mood

Music is so emotive – it can make you smile, relax, dance, or even cry.

You will probably have tunes that can transport you to the best and worst times of your life. The soundtrack of your history – the school discos, the break-up songs, and the love songs.

You can create playlists that will quickly lift your spirits and make you smile, laugh and dance. Choose what will be on your positive playlist to your bag.

My feelgood tunes are...

1.

2.

3.

4.

5.

Take time later to actually create your playlist on a CD or other device. Listen to it and add to it, dance to it – who cares if someone is watching!

Laughter really is the best medicine

Children laugh over 300 times a day, adults about 15, according to studies.But a good laugh really makes you feel good – it releases endorphins and feelgood chemicals, it's good for your heart, and lowers stress.

Laughter lifts your mood and allows you to connect more easily with other people.

Create a laughter bank – which you can take out on a rainy day! What makes you laugh? Gather the dvds, the books, the jokes, all together – add the list to your bag.

My laughter bank contains...

1.

2

3.

4.

5.

Now put your laughter collection together in one handy place so that it is easy to find.

Dreams can come true

Do you have a bucket list? You know, the list of things that you want to do before you die?

No? Then now is the time to make one. Let your imagination run riot: what would you really like to do? Are there places you want to visit? Experiences you want to try out? Maybe you want to change career, live in another place, learn some new skills.

Take a few minutes and write whatever comes to mind. Let your ideas flow unchallenged – no 'if only' or 'I can't do it'.

My dreams....

1.

2.

3.

4.

5.

Always leave space to add more.

Actions speak louder than words

Dreams are great, but often they stay that way – as dreams. Setting goals gives your dream legs, then they can actually go somewhere!

Pick one of your dreams from the previous exercise. Ask yourself, what can I do today to begin this journey? What steps can I take that will start this off?

My dream is...

First step I can take...

Commit yourself to that first step. Now, close your eyes and imagine that you are taking that step: make it real, see yourself doing it. Doesn't it feel good?

Now keep going. Add more steps and begin to actually live your dreams.

Kindness is good for you

One of the best ways to increase your own happiness is to do something for another person. Now that you are focussed on feeling good, it's time to pass that feeling on.

What can you do to be kind to others? Pay your good feelings forward. If someone does something good for you, then thank them, but say you will pay it forward by doing a good deed for another person.

Acts of kindness can be small things, too – a smile, a kind word, even a cup of tea!

What acts of kindness can you commit to doing?

1.

2.

3.

4.

5.

Continue to add more kindness to your day.

It's your special place

This is your Bag of Happiness; you can add anything you want to it.

Some people have put in photos, cards or special mementoes. One person filled hers with bouncy balls!

The bag is yours to add to. Whenever you recognise something that makes you feel good, you can add it to your bag.

Think of it as your own private supply of sunshine; a bag of positive energy. With every deposit, you will gain 'interest' by seeing your happiness continue to grow.

Now what?

Okay, so you have filled your bag. Great – what do you do with it?

You must carry this around with you forever!!! At least, inside your head. You will never forget making your own Bag of Happiness; it's in your memory, so you can access it whenever you like.

Take notice of the fun, happy moments in your life. Keep adding them to your bag as you go through the years.

If you feel low, are stressed, or going through a difficult time, just get your bag and take out the items. Remember those happy memories, what you are proud of, the things you like about yourself, and immerse yourself in them. Play your playlist; withdraw something from your laughter bank. Play a little. You can use any, or all, of the items in your bag to connect with your positive mindset.

Some things work better at different times, so keep going. You will begin to feel happier, you will notice that your mood lifts, and the world seems a different place.

Once you have bounced back, take another look at your problems – they may seem less stressful, or maybe you will be able to find a solution easier.

You have created your very own Bag of Happiness to treasure, but you have also found a way to build resilience and a positive mindset. I truly hope that you have enjoyed this process.

Choose to connect with as many positive people as you can. Share your happiness and theirs; it really makes a difference. My Happiness Clubs offer an opportunity to do that on a regular monthly basis.

Check out if there is Happiness Club near you. You can continue to learn new ways to beat the low times and feel good.

Keep up the good work.

I wish you good health, wealth and happiness,

Kim Macleod

If you have any questions or comments please contact me

kim@stressthepostiive.co.uk

Twitter @stresspositive

www.facebook.com/StressthePositive

Lightning Source UK Ltd.
Milton Keynes UK
UKOW06f1420260415

250344UK00010B/60/P